THE
DISTRACTIONS
OF PERSECUTION
& TRIBULATION
It's Only a Distraction

REGINALD EZELL

Trafford rev. 09/09/2020

www.trafford.com
North America & international
toll-free: 844-688-6899 (USA & Canada)
fax: 812 355 4082

Contents

Foreword

It is becoming clearer in these last days that Satan is doing everything he can to keep God's children from obtaining the promise of His blessings. This is the time to walk in God's exceeding abundance. The Word says God is *"...able to do exceedingly abundantly above all that we ask or think, according to the power that worketh in us..." (Ephesians 3:20)*.

But what is this power that's working in us? When we accepted Jesus Christ, the Anointed One and His anointing, and became born again, we activated His power to work through us. We also have the Holy Ghost Who knows the mind of Christ and intercedes on our behalf when we speak in tongues. Then there are assigned angels who hearken to the voice of the Word (Psalms 103:20). Every time we speak the Word of God, they are obligated to carry out the assignment. Therefore, we have everything we need to win.

Satan knows this, but all too often we forget and allow circumstances to distract us. God has given us the authority to use the name of Jesus to remove every burden and to destroy every yoke. God encourages us to cast our cares on Him (1Peter 5:7), and He also promised us that He will fight every battle. The Bible says in 2 Chronicles 20:15 *"...be not afraid nor dismayed.... for the battle is not yours, but God's"*

In this thought-provoking book, Reginald Ezell challenges us to be mindful of this simple truth-God is in control. The Distraction or Persecution and Tribulation is a must read. As my dear son in the ministry, I am truly proud of this anointed work. The knowledge revealed herein will not only change your life, but it will give you the fuel you need to victoriously walk through every battle, and recognize the devil for what he is -a minor distraction!

Dr. Creflo A Dollar
Senior Pastor and Founder
World Changers Church Intl

Chapter 1

Satan's
Scheme

"Quitting is not an Option"

Reference: Galatians 6:9

To begin to understand that tribulation and persecution is only a distraction, you must first realize what these things are and from where they come. We know that confusion; temptation, frustration, and dissolution are works of the devil. We also know that these things are the results of tribulation and persecution. It doesn't take a great deal of deductive reasoning to determine that tribulation and persecution is from Satan.

With that understanding, let's begin by laying a solid foundation. First, it is necessary to recognize and discern the Plot and uncover Satan's scheme. We must understand how he works and what he does. His motive is to distract us and get our attention off what God has done, what God is doing, and what we believe God will do in our lives.

We cannot assume that knowing who the enemy is will be enough. It is more important to know who you are. You must be fully aware of who you are and what you have in God. Let's begin laying the foundation by looking at Ephesians 2: 11-13,19.

"Wherefore remember, that ye being in time past that Gentiles in the flesh, who are called Uncircumcision by that Which is called the Circumcision in the flesh made by hands; That at that time ye were without Christ, being aliens from the commonwealth of Israel, and strangers from the covenants of promise, having no hope, and without God in the world: But now in Christ Jesus ye who sometimes were far off are made nigh by the blood of Christ. Now therefore ye are no **more strangers and foreigners, but fellow citizens with the saints, and of the household of God"**

You must understand what the blood of Jesus has done. It has enabled us to be a part of the covenant of God. That is why you must study the Word of God. The Word is not intended to establish anything. It is to let us know what has already been established. It shows us what is in that covenant, what God said when He cut the covenant, what we have been born into, and the whole purpose of God in the establishment of the covenant. It tells us who we are and what we have. It is important that we become covenant-minded. This requires us to have our minds renewed. We cannot do this alone. It is the Word of God that renews our minds.

Chapter 2

Renewing
Our Mind

"We teach what we know, but we reproduce who we are"

Reference: Genesis 1:11-25

Ephesians 4:22,23 states,

"That ye put off, concerning the former conversation, the old man, which is corrupt according to the deceitful lusts.... And be ye renewed in the spirit of your mind."

To truly understand who we are and what God did for us, we must know who we were, where we came from, understand what Adam did, and how his actions affected us.

When Adam was created, God commanded that he be fruitful and multiply. He commanded that everything reproduce after its own kind. Keep that law in mind as we explain further. If Adam had borne children before he sinned, while he was still pure and totally connected to God, his children would have been born children of the light of God. They would have been born of the spirit and not of the flesh.

It is important to understand that when Adam sinned, certain new laws and commandments went into operation. However, the old laws were not done away with. Everything still produced after its own kind. When Adam sinned, that sin Nature was passed to his seed. All that were born after Adam sinned were born into that sin nature. That is not to say that everyone sins willfully from the womb.

Let's look at it practically. If your father and mother have red hair and freckles, and their parents and grandparents had red hair and freckles, guess what you'll have? It does not come by any act on your part. It is a part of your family's nature. Because of this law of reproduction, all born of Adam after he sinned were born into his sinful nature. To inherit that red hair all you had to do was be born. To inherit Adam's sin nature, you only have to be born. That's why it took Jesus, not born of man's seed, to redeem man from the curse of sin and death. If he had been born of man's sperm, He would have been as corrupt as every other man. It is that redemption paid for by the pure, innocent blood of Jesus that gives us victory over this world and the wiles of Satan to distract us. We must renew our minds to this truth.

God puts emphasis on the need for us to renew our minds because that sin nature that I just described keeps us sin conscious. We are conscious of our sin and we allow Satan to use his maneuvers and tactics to distract us from the truth of who we are in Christ. We believe that Satan is the power of this world and that he has power over us. We often say, "The devil made me do it." No, you did it because you wanted to. You have the power to resist the devil and conquer his schemes, but you must first renew your mind.

Romans 12:2 reads,

"And be not conformed to this world, but be ye Transformed by the renewing of your mind; that ye may prove what is that good and acceptable and perfect will of God."

Even though Satan is the god of this world, you don't have to conform yourself to the world system. You can overcome it. If we allow the things of the world to dictate what we choose, we will be caught up in the things of Satan. We become too easily distracted. Not thinking about and conforming to the world system allows us to concentrate on being renewed by the things of God.

We must also understand what Satan inherited at that time. He has free reign on this earth and in the air above the earth. The Word calls him the prince and power of the air. He inherited man's ability to have dominion over all the earth and every creeping thing that crept upon the earth. When man lost favor with God and that constant dependence on God's leadership and guidance, Satan gained the entrance to deceive. When Adam was created he depended on God for everything and every decision. The good and bad that he knew came from the throne of God. Only God knew what was right and wrong and all of Adam's decisions were based on God's will.

After he ate of the fruit of the knowledge of good and evil, his decisions were his own. He believed that he could distinguish between good and evil and those decisions were made totally apart from God. This was the very root of tribulation and persecution. Through this act of disobedience, man gave Satan access to the area around the throne of God. He could freely go to and from about the earth and present evil reports to God. It is important to know that he did not, however, have access to the throne of God. That is vital, beloved. Remember that we are renewing our minds and laying the foundation.

Chapter 3

We are
Free Moral
Agents

"Don't tell me what you can't do, just tell me what you don't want to do, because when you want to do it, you will find a way"

Reference: Matthew 6:21

We have discussed what happened to Adam's seed and what happened to Satan. It is important to know what and whose we are. God created us as free moral agents. God didn't want millions of robots programmed to love and serve Him. He gave us a choice. Abraham had a choice. He had the right to choose or not to choose God. In the covenant, God told Abraham that if he chose to serve, obey and follow Him, that He would be his God. God knew that Abraham had that right to choose. Fortunately, for the people of faith, Abraham made the right choice. God gave us a choice – that same choice!

The Word states in Deuteronomy 30:19,

"I call heaven and earth to record this day against you, that I have set before you life and death, blessing and cursing: therefore choose life, that both thou and thy seed may live."

It is important for you to understand what this means to you today. Because Abraham had the right to choose, and passed the blessing of making the right choice to his seed, you have that right to those blessings, too. Satan *could not* stop him from making the right choice and God definitely *would not* stop him. The same exists today. Satan cannot stop you from choosing God as your God. Once you choose Him, He fight your battles. Satan may be the price and power of the air and the god of this world, but God says that He will be your God. Satan had and has no power even after Adam had turned over authority to him. Satan had nothing in his power to stop Abraham from making his decision to serve God. And the good news is that neither does he have power over your decision to choose God now.

The average person believes that being a free moral agent means that we can do whatever we want and that no one can make us do anything different. But remember you're not average, you are a child of the covenant. You must become covenant minded. You are a free moral agent so that you can choose God's protection, protection from every plot and plan of Satan, including persecution and tribulation.

Because the things of God have already been established, we must make up our minds to commit ourselves to those things and not the things of Satan. Satan can't stop us. his weapons are only to distract us from this truth.

Romans 12:2 says,

"And be not conformed to this world: but be ye transformed by the renewing of your mind, that you may prove what is that good, and acceptable, and perfect, will of God."

Because you are born of this world you must decide to transform your mind. The Word of God must transform your thinking. Although you were born into the world, you can be transformed by renewing your mind to the new man that you became when you were born again in Christ Jesus.

The sin nature of man is still in this world. This gives Satan lawful reign in the world. But your spirit is of God. It belongs to God. It is led of the things of the Spirit and not the things of the world. As a free moral agent, must decide whether to let your body be led by your old mind or your new spirit, and he knows that. That is why he attacks your old man.

To be an overcomer in this life, you must forsake the old man and submit yourself to the new man that is led by God. When you submit yourself to God, you resist the devil, and he will flee from you. What is Satan after anyway? He is not after you or even your new man. He is after the Jesus on the inside of you. What did Satan want from the beginning? He wanted to exalt himself above God so that all creation would worship him. He wants that which God created- that which God loves and holds precious- to worship him. What does God hold most precious -Jesus. Because you are a part of the Body of Christ you are precious to God. Satan wants to keep your mind off of those things that God has purposed for your life. Just like in the beginning, he doesn't want God to get the glory out of your life. As we renew our mind with the Word of God, Satan will have no place in our lives. We can be led by the Sprit and not be conformed to this world- Satan's world of tribulation, persecution and distraction.

Does this mean that we will never suffer persecution or tribulation? Let's see what the Word says. In 2 Timothy 3:12, it says, *"Yea and all that will live godly in Christ Jesus shall suffer persecution."* The word *suffer* does not mean", to put up with, to fall under or to be overcome by." It means to hold up, to stand strong under the pressure. The good news is that we know from whence our strength comes; therefore, we should hold up and stand strong. Nehemiah 8 tells us that the joy of the Lord is our strength. We can and must find joy in the face of all adversity, tribulation, and distraction, in the fact that God is in complete control and that He has already overcome the world. Take joy in the fact that He has overcome every situation in your life.

Chapter 4

Knowing
What
God has
Established

"It's not if it happen, but when it happens; For it shall surely come to pass"

Reference: Isaiah 55:11,

We have established the foundation of who we are, what God intended, what Satan gained in the garden, and the limits of his power. We understand that even with all that he received from Adam, Satan could not stop Abraham from making a decision to serve God and to make God his God. He could not stop the prophets from making a decision to do God's will. It was the same with the children of Israel. From time to time, he swayed their mind, but their ultimate decision was to trust God and they reached the Promised Land. Every step of the way, they had a choice. God provided for them and protected their choice. The same applies to you. You are a free moral agent with the ability to choose. Satan can't and God won't make that choice for you. You must make a choice.

Hosea 4:6 tells us that, **"...my people are destroyed for lack of knowledge."** Knowledge of what? He is referring to the knowledge of what has already been established. He is not referring to what lies before you or what is yet to be established in your life but what has already been established in heaven and on the earth. Satan uses that ignorance to sway us in directions that have not been established nor predestined for us to walk in. God has laid out the path and laid all of our blessings in that path.

Because we are not knowledgeable of His will for our lives, we aim in different directions hitting here and missing there. We end up in situations and miss many blessings. It is so necessary to renew our minds to discern those things that God has established. We must know the gospel of Jesus Christ-the promises for us that were wrapped up in Him-so that we can walk in the assurance and direction of God.

To accomplish this, He gave us the Holy Spirit to dwell on the inside of us and to lead and guide us. Even with this precious power, we can still make the wrong decisions and choices in which the Holy Spirit has no part. He comes as a Helper. He helps us in our infirmities and our weaknesses. When we don't know which way to go, He leads us gently by reminding us of what the Word of God says about the situation. Yet, sometimes that is only when we ask. The decisions are ultimately ours to make. He will tell us what is not the right way to go, and therefore direct us in a different way. But all too often, we make our own independent decisions–independent of where God is leading us and subsequently walk out on our own. Once we get out there and experience trouble in our lives, we tend to focus on the situation and circumstances and try to figure out on our own how to get back on track.

That is exactly what Satan wants. This is how God's people are destroyed. The lack of knowledge about the covenant, about being free moral agents and our right and ability to choose, and about Satan's inability to stop us from choosing God, creates distractions. Persecution, afflictions and tribulations are only distractions to get our focus off the things of God. They distract us from the path where all of our blessings lie.

Our first step in avoiding these distractions is to change the way we look at what God has already told us in His Word. Let's begin to look at the promises, knowing that we have the choice to receive them and that Satan can't keep the promises from manifesting in our lives.

In John 16:33 Jesus tells us, **"These things I have spoken unto you, that in me ye might have peace. In the world ye shall have tribulation: but be of good cheer; I have overcome the world."** He is saying, that He has overcome all the things that will come to distract you. So, don't worry about it, just be happy. He is telling us that we can overcome because He has overcome. In this, He is our living example; He has already overcome Distractions for us. Now we can walk as overcomers.

Chapter 5

Christ Our Example

"Best is the Seed to Better and Better is the Process to Best"

Reference: Colossians 3:23

Let's look at the example He set for us knowing that because He did, we can.

Philippians 4:13 says, **"I can do all things through Christ which strengthened me."** We gain strength through the knowledge of what He has done and promised. Satan tempted Jesus in everything, just as he does to us, yet Jesus did not fall. However, many of us say that He couldn't fall because He was God. The Word tells us in Hebrews 4:15 **"For we have not a high priest which cannot be touched with the feeling of our infirmities; but was in all points tempted like as we are, yet without sin."** He made a quality decision and said. **"I only do that which my father says to do and only say that which my father tells me to say."** He told Satan, **"it's not my will, but the will of Him who sent me."**

Jesus made it clear to Satan that He had made a decision. His mind was made up. He had no intention to fall. He knew that the promise of His father was sure. Having taken His stand all the way to the cross, He rose with the keys of all authority in His hand. This was significant. All of the authority that was handed to Satan in the garden was returned to its rightful owner, God. And in Christ, it is yours. Not only do you have authority to make the right choices, you have the power and authority over all that pertains to life and godliness. You now have authority and dominion over the heavens, the earth and everything under the earth. Satan is the god of this world system and the prince of the power of the air, but we have power over him. Satan no longer has the power to distract you unless you let him.

The Bible says that the devil now goes about as a roaring lion seeking whom he may devour and destroy (1 Peter 5:8). Let's understand how lions work to get a picture of what Satan is attempting today in this earth. Lions run in packs. They sit back and watch a whole group of animals. They watch their patterns and their movements. They search out easy prey. They target the slower, weaker animals.

Smart animals like gazelles and deer know the wiles of the lions. They have learned to run and leap. Their leaping exhibits strength, fitness and agility. Their goal is to make the lions believe that they will not be easy prey. They want the lions to know that they will have to work hard for that meal.

Because this is exactly what Satan is doing, we must grow up in faith. When he comes looking for easy prey, we must stand strong. We can't stand strong enough in our own strength or might. We must stand strong in the Lord. The devil must see that we are in covenant with God and that he has no place in our lives. He will quickly decide that there is easier prey out there than you. He will continue to search for someone he can devour because it won't be you. He will find someone else on which to inflict persecution.

Chapter 6

The Decision and The Seed

"If people, situation, and circumstances have that much influence in your life, then it's because God doesn't have enough"

Reference: Roman 6:12–16

Your strong stand in God begins with your decision. Remember you are a free moral agent. Let's review the origins of your choice by examining Abraham's options and his decision. In Deuteronomy 30:19, God charges us by setting life and death before us and tells us to **"choose life, that both thou and thy seed may live."** Abraham made a choice that established prosperity for himself and his seed. That was God's purpose and plan.

Before Abram was asked to make a decision and before he was given a promise, God told him to leave his father's house and his kindred. Decisions may affect your family. God did not want any of the decisions Abram's father made to affect Abram's future or the future of his seed. Obviously, God had big plans for the seed of Abraham. Praise God for those plans which impact our lives today! But the fulfillment of all of those plans was hinged on Abraham's decision. In Genesis 17:7, God promised Abraham that the blessings would be upon him and his seed. If Abraham chose to walk before God and be perfect, God promised to, **"establish my covenant between me and thee and thy seed after thee in their generations for an everlasting covenant, to be a God unto thee, and to thy seed after thee."**

God was looking for someone who would make a quality decision to make God his God so that He could show Himself strong through him and his seed. Our blessings as Abraham's seed came through that quality decision that he made.

That decision brought forth God's blessings, His protection and His grace. When Abraham declared God as his God, God supplied everything that declaration required. God took responsibility for man and his family. No longer could Satan be Abraham's god. No longer did he have power over Abraham's life. God was able to have His way—that better way—in Abraham's life.

It can be the same in your life. When you make that same decision-to make God your God and give Him control of your life–Satan can no longer have power in your life or your family. The decision is yours.

You must understand that Satan cannot keep you from making that decision. And once it is made, he can no longer distract you unless you let him. As the seed of Abraham, you have a covenant with God. He is responsible for your life, prosperity, health and your family as a part of that covenant. That covenant contains promises about all of these things. How do we tap into these things and avoid those distractions? Making quality decisions doesn't keep Satan from trying to distract us with tribulation and persecution. Jesus told us in John 16:33, **"In the world ye shall have tribulation: but be of good cheer; I have overcome the world."**

Chapter 7

Seek Ye
First

"True Success is not everyone changing to conform to what you want or believe, it's you changing to where they don't affect you."

Reference: I Corinthians 15:58

Unsaved people often seek the blessings of God. They seek the things of this world—wealth, health, houses and land. They seek these things without seeking God. The Word explains plainly that "all things are of God" and that the earth is the Lord's and the fullness thereof. Unlike the unsaved, it is impossible for believers to seek and receive these things without first seeking the One who gives them. **"But seek ye first the kingdom of God, and His righteousness; and all these things shall be added unto you"** Matthew 6:33. Once you make the decision to let God be your God and to seek Him first, God will add all of these things to you. The Things are a distraction from Satan when we seek them without seeking God first. He knows what we have need of and He is a rewarder of those that diligently seek Him (Hebrews 11:6). He set before us blessings and cursing and told us to choose. With that choice, we not only have Jesus and the Holy Spirit but the provision of clothes, food and shelter as well. If you are hungry and naked and without peace, you are either walking in the curse, having not made the decision for God, or are seeking the things and not seeking God. In either case, these things are a distraction.

Jesus knew this. That is why He told His disciples to feed and clothe men in need and then preach the gospel to them. Hunger, nakedness and lack of shelter will distract anyone from hearing the Word they need for their deliverance. How can they seek God in whom they have not heard? How can they hear when they are distracted by the cares of this world. Satan knows this too. The good news is—now so do you.

Jesus came that we might have life and have it more abundantly (John 10:10). What the thief seeks to steal and destroy is that abundant life. He cannot touch your life or your health (we will discuss these issues in the next chapter) but he can destroy the peace and prosperity or your abundant life by distracting you from the things of God.

Your quality decision for God stops Satan in his tracks. Your decision has all the power of the living God backing it up. God will protect the decisions you make when the decisions are based on His Word. Your decisions place you in the arena of faith. This is where you win or lose. Imagine the games of the ancient Roman and Egyptian empires when men were thrown into lion's dens. Remember, Satan goes about as a roaring lion and he is the god of this world. Also remember that you are in this world but not of this world and that you have all of God's power backing you if you make the right decision. Don't you want that awesome power in the arena with you? Daniel knew what it meant to walk into the den with that power. So, did David. And so, you can too. Just make the right decision.

Chapter 8

God's Word Works -It's Established

"Without the question asked, you will not be mindful of the answer and you won't benefit from the solution"

Reference: James 4:2-3

In chapter 4, we discussed the covenant that God established. However, we did not talk about His word. In Matthew 18:16, we learn that "IN THE MOUTH OF TWO OR THREE WITNESSES EVERY WORD MAY BE ESTABLISHED." In Isaiah 55:11 God tells us; **"So shall my word be that goeth forth out of my mouth: it shall not return unto me void, but it shall accomplish that which I please, and that it shall prosper in the thing whereto I send it."** His Word is established in Heaven and here on this earth. When we truly believe that it is established in our lives, we will be able to combat the persecutions and tribulations that come into our lives to distract us.

The word "establish" means; to make firm, to purpose, to make stand solid, to create. God did not speak His word just to be heard, but to be established. That ability to establish His word is the power of His word. In days long past, men understood the value of this principle. A man's word was his bond because a man was bound to establish his word. Today, many people are not worthy of trust because they take their words so lightly, that principle has been abandoned. But it is not so with God.

When God spoke it, He established it. This has been true since the beginning and it still exists today. God said, "I change not." Since this is true, (and it is), then His established Word has not changed nor has that which He established changed. He spoke the words, **"Let there be light:"** (Genesis 3:3) and it has established. He said that the seed of the woman (Jesus) shall bruise thy head (Satan) and it was established. Jesus was God in the flesh and what He said, He also established.

Proof of that is found in John 8 when Jesus said only what He heard His Father say. What He spoke was the Word of God and He and the Father had the authority to establish every word. In John 14:12 Jesus said**,... "the works that I do shall he do also: and greater**

works than these shall he do"; That was established. He told us that He gave us the power to tread on serpents and scorpions, to lay our hands on the sick and they would recover, to speak with new tongues, to cast out devils and that no deadly thing could harm us. Those things are established and can be true today in your life.

Chapter 9

So Easily
Distracted –
3 Case
Studies

"Avoidance is not Victory; Neither a way of Escape"

Reference: I Corinthians 10:13

A s we learn the Word of God and it's power then we begin to see where we have missed it – and God—in the past, and we get very frustrated and say, "How did I let Satan distract me?" Remember that the Word says, there is nothing new under the sun and that there are brothers of like-faith all over this world experiencing the same afflictions that you do. Let me show you three such examples. These are three men of great faith who became easily distracted. Throughout this chapter keep in mind that God's Word has been established for yesterday, today and tomorrow.

Abraham Takes His Eyes off the Promise In Genesis 12, God promised Abram a seed and not just a seed but a great nation of offspring. Abram believed the Lord and set out for the land that God would show him. After much travel and many victories, he was distracted by what he saw. Actually, he was distracted by what he didn't see.

In Genesis 15:2, Abram said, **"Lord God, what wilt thou give me, seeing I go childless, and the steward of mine house is Eliezer of Damascus. To me thou hast given no seed: and lo, one born in my house is mine heir"**. He took his eyes off God's promise of a seed and he focused on what he saw. God reassured him that his seed would come from his bowels and cut covenant with him. Once again, Abram believed.

Shortly thereafter, Abram again saw that his wife had no child. This time she distracted him and suggested that he mate with her maid. When Ishmael was born, Abram presented him to God, **"O that Ishmael might live before thee."** God reminded him of His promise of a son to him and Sarai.

God changed their names as reassurance and, once again, Abraham believed. This time he refused to be distracted by Sarah's disbelieving laughter. He would not be again distracted or disappointed. **"He believed God and it was counted to him for righteousness."**

Twenty-six years and three distractions later, he received his son, and he became the Father of faith and many nations.

Moses Looks at the People and Missed the Promised Land God chose Moses to lead the children of Israel out of bondage. He promised to lead him and directed their every step through the pillar of cloud by day and pillar of fire by night. Moses focused on the word of the Lord and led the people. He was not distracted by their murmuring and complaining or his own family's rebellion. In Numbers 20, the people again spoke against God. Moses and Aaron demanded water. As He always acted when the people complained, God gave Moses a word to keep him focused on Him.

This time Moses let the people distract him. He did not heed God's direction and smote the rock instead of speaking to it to bring forth water. The people received their water. But for their disobedience, Moses and Aaron never entered into the promised land. In Numbers 20:12 **"the Lord spoke unto Moses and Aaron, because ye believed me not, to sanctify me in the eyes of the children of Israel, therefore ye shall not bring this congregation into the land which I have given them."** They both died before they entered in to the promised land.

Beloved, do not get discouraged. God always makes His promise good. He promised Moses that he would lead his people to the promised land and that he would see it. He did just that. He led them to its borders and he looked over and saw it. He just was not allowed to enter in. God's promise to him, just like Abraham's, was fulfilled. And He will fulfill His promise to you.

Peter walks on water

When Jesus called Peter to come, He was promising him safety on the water if he would not be afraid. As long as he kept his focus and eyes on Jesus, Peter was able to walk on the water. He then got distracted by what he saw–the winds and the waves. He began to sink. Jesus reached out His hand and saved him. Just as the Word of God tell us in Psalms 37:24, *"Though he fall, he shall not be utterly cast down: for the Lord upholdeth him with his hand",* even if you get distracted (as these three men did), the Lord will uphold and restore you. Praise God for His divine wisdom and mercy.

These stories reveal the fact that Abraham's doubt, Moses' anger and Peter's fear entered in and became distractions to them. They let the distractions delay the manifestation of the promises. Satan, the author of doubt, anger and fear, may delay, but He cannot stop God's plan. God's plan is established. Once we begin to operate in faith again, after being distracted, it must come to pass. Remember that God's word (His promise to you), is established. We have that same creative ability to establish those things that we speak. Too often, we speak doubt, anger and fear. We just need to walk in those things that God has already established for us.

"What people hear they understand, what they see they believe"

Reference: John 14:10-11

Chapter 10

Nothing
Shall
Separate Us

"If you are not convinced, then you will not be convincing"

Reference: I John 3:20-21

By now, you know that God's Word and His promises to you are an established truth. Nothing that Satan throws your way can change that. Satan is a defeated foe. That is the first established fact. Let us build this chapter's revelations from that point. You are a child of God. Would your heavenly Father give you a stone if you asked for bread? Let us believe Him for His divine wisdom regarding His established promises in our lives.

Once you make a quality decision to submit your life to God and believe that He is able to do just what He has said, Satan will have no power in your life and his tricks will not distract you. If you are governed by your senses–what you feel, see, hear, taste or touch–you are not being led by the Spirit of God, the Spirit of truth, which has been established. Even distractions are temporal. They still cannot permanently separate you from the promises of God. Remember, you are a child of God.

Romans 8:35-36 says, **"Who shall separate us from the love of Christ? Shall tribulation or distress, or persecution, or famine, or nakedness, or peril or sword?** FOR THY SAKE WE ARE KILLED ALL THE DAY LONG; WE ARE ACCOUNTED AS SHEEP FOR THE SLAUGHTER."** However, verse 37 tells us no because, **"in all things we are more than conquerors through Him that loved us."** Why? Psalm 44:17 tells us that, **"All this is come upon us; yet have we not forgotten thee, neither have we dealt falsely in thy covenant."** In other words, we have continued to believe that God's Word is established.

We must believe that neither death, nor life, nor principalities, nor powers, nor things present, nor things to come, nor height, nor depth, nor any other creature, shall be able to separate us from the love of God, which is in Jesus Christ our Lord. He said **nothing!** You must understand that everything contrary to this established Word is a distraction.

When you make that quality decision to let God be God in your life, nothing can separate you. Being laid off from your job or unemployed has nothing to do with the established truth in Philippians 4:19, **"But my God shall supply all your need according to His riches in glory by Christ Jesus."** Everything Contrary to that truth is just a distraction. When you walk in God's truth, it is established. God must meet all your needs.

You have been diagnosed with a headache or terminal cancer. Both are contrary to the Word in Isaiah 53:5, **"With His stripes we are healed."** The doctor's report has nothing to do with the established truth that you (walking in the Spirit), are healed. Satan cannot prevent your healing. He can only delay it through distraction which causes doubt and unbelief. You must make the decision to accept your healing which has already been established.

When you find yourself under constant attack by others, remember that Isaiah 54:17 promises that, **"No weapon that is formed against thee shall prosper; and every tongue that shall rise against thee in judgement thou shalt condemn..."** That is your inheritance. That is yours once you have made the decision to let God fight your battles. It is in the will. Everything contrary to that truth is a distraction. Claim your inheritance now. Walk in all that belongs to you as a servant and a son or daughter of God.

Chapter 11

You are More Than Able!

"It's what you refuse to change in that keeps you from going to the next level in God"

Reference: Philippian 3:12-14

When persecution and tribulation come in our lives, the first thing most Christian say is "Why Me". Some Christians even think that the persecution and tribulation indicate that what they are doing is not the will of God. I truly believe in most cases it's the complete opposite. Why would the devil come to stop you from going in the wrong direction? In Mark 4:14-14 says, **"The sower sowth the word. And these are they by the way side, where the word is sown; but when they have heard, Satan cometh immediately, and taketh away the word that was sown in their hearts."**

In this scripture, we see that Satan comes for the word that was sown and not for the word that will be sown. This is good to know for two reasons. First, the word sown in your life is for God's direction for you. In other words, it's Gods' steps for you so that you can get to your expected end. Secondly, with the word sown in your life comes God's ability to accomplish His will and overcome every persecution and tribulation in your life. The second reason is what I want to talk about. 2 Corinthians 3:5-6 says, *"Not that we are sufficient of ourselves to think any thing as of ourselves; but our sufficiency is of God; Who also hath made us able ministers of the new testament; not of the letter, but of the spirit: for the letter killeth, but the spirit giveth life."*

Here we see that our ability comes from God's spirit in us and not of ourselves. God's word gives us an understanding of God's ability in us. God made us able ministers and not ourselves. We must trust God's word and have faith and confidence in Him. Proverb 3:5 say, *"Trust in the Lord with all thine heart; and lean not unto thine own understanding."* Hebrew 10:22-23 says, *"Let us draw near with a true heart in full assurance of faith, having our hearts sprinkled from an evil conscience, and our bodies washed with pure water. Let us hold fast the profession of our faith without wavering: (for he is faithful that promised).* Hebrew 10:35-39 say: *Cast not away therefore your confidence, which hath great recompence of reward. For ye have need of patience, that, after ye have done the will of God, ye might receive the promise.* These scriptures show us the important of trust, faith and confidence in our life for God's word.

One main thing I don't believe most Christians realize is that the word you have or the word that has been sown in you is for you right where you are. The word that you will get is for where you are going. You have enough in you to conquer or overcome anything you're going through. 1 Corinthians 10:13 says, *"There hath no temptation taken you but shall as is common to man: But God is faithful, who will not suffer you to be tempted above that ye are able; but will with the temptation also make a way to escape. That ye may be able to bear it.*

First thing we see in this scripture is, what ever you are going through someone else has already gone through before. However, the key thought is "gone through". The attack Satan brings is nothing new and it's not more than you can handle. The scripture says, "He will not suffer you to be tempted above that ye are able. You are ABLE. Inspite of what the Devil says or what you think you are able to conquer, overcome, master, defeat, or win in whatever you are going through. I have a saying when I minister, and it is, "If the shoe fit take them off, you don't want to wear those shoes and if it don't apply to you don't let it bother you, but a hit dog holler the loudest". The reason I share this is because one of the silliest things I've seen is when it's raining hard in an area people pull over in their cars and stop to wait the rain out, and a hundred yards down the road it's not raining and if they would just press through with caution, but don't stop, it may only be raining in the small area ahead. This is the same attitude you should take when it come to the tribulation and persecution in your life. I'm not going to pitch a tent and set up camp. But I will go through and see the end of God's promises in my life. Galatians 6:9 says, *"and let us not be weary in well doing: For in due season we shall reap, it we faint not"* if we don't give up, cave in, or quit". Know that God's Spirit in you gives you the ability to win in this road of life.

I John 4:4 say, *"Ye are of God, little children, and have overcome them: Because greater is He that is in you, than he that is in the world.* We know Satan is the god of this world's system, but the spirit of God in you is greater than the enemy. The spirit of God in you carries God' Anointed power to do. That same Anointing lives in us. The scripture my ministry was founded on is Philippians 4:13 which says, *"I can do all things through Christ which strengthenth me."* I want to share this same scripture from the amplified version of the bible to give a greater understanding of who lives in you. It says, *"I have strength for all things in Christ who empowers me [I am ready for anything through Him who infuses inner strength into me: I am self-sufficient in Christ's sufficiency]* the price that Jesus paid and the gift that God gave to you in the form of the Holy Spirit makes you able to do and overcome Satan's distractions.

"Arise, Shine, for thy light is come, and the glory of the Lord is risen upon thee." That is your promise in Isaiah 60:1. Anything else is just a distraction. **Amen!!**

Reginald Ezell

Reginald Ezell is an author, conference speaker, entrepreneur and pastor. He is known for his teachings on leadership, servanthood and ministry of helps. He and his wife, Wanta founded World Covenant Christian Center in Conyers, Georgia in 2006. Reginald's other books includes, A Heart to Serve, Developing the Complete You, and The Five Talent Man.

Reginald Ezell resides with his family in Social Circle, Georgia.

For more information on Reginald Ezell, follow him on @reginaldezellministries.

To order this book and other materials offered by Reginald Ezell or if you would like to become a partner with Reginald Ezell Ministries, you can write to:

REGINALD EZELL MINISTRIES
45 Surrey Chase Dr
Social Circle GA 30025

Printed in the United States
By Bookmasters